THE CEO'S STORY VAULT

Volume 1

Shannon Park

Zollars

Author Bio

Shannon Park is a leadership communication coach, business English expert, Korean-English interpreter, and the founder of **Collars Language & Leadership Lab**.

With over 15 years of experience empowering global leaders — including CEOs of global companies — she specializes in helping them articulate ideas with clarity, credibility, and authentic voice in English.

At Collars, she equips senior leaders with the language and presence to lead across borders.

Her clients span Korea's top conglomerates, global consulting firms, and high-profile international initiatives — including the 2018 PyeongChang Winter Olympic Bid Committee.

Shannon holds an M.A. in Korean-English Translation from the Middlebury Institute of International Studies in California and a Law degree from Sungkyunkwan University.

She has delivered thousands of hours of coaching, interpretation, and strategic content across the worlds *of corporate leadership, international negotiation, legal documentation, and televised media.*

From the boardroom to the broadcast studio, her work has always centered on one essential question:

How can leaders speak so they are truly heard — across languages, across cultures, and in moments that matter most?

And just as importantly, she has always asked herself:

How can I help leaders speak with fluency, but with real influence?

This book is her answer.

Preface

Why I Wrote This Book

There's a moment most leaders dread: When someone turns to you in a meeting and says, "So what's your take on this?" The spotlight hits. The room quiets. And your mind... races.

You know you have something to say — but will it land?

After years of coaching CEOs in business English, I've come to a simple, powerful realization: No matter what textbook or article we start with, the real magic only happens when a leader takes the content, internalizes it, and turns it into their own story — in the first person, in the right context, at the right moment.

But I also realized something else. There were no materials out there to help leaders do exactly that.

Not a workbook. Not a script. A vault — of ready-made, high-trust stories that leaders could **inhabit**, **retell**, *and* **make their own**.

So I created one.

This book isn't about learning English. It's about embodying leadership in English — with stories you can use in town halls, tough conversations, board meetings, or simply with yourself.

Each chapter includes a first-person business story, key expressions, leadership reflection, and a practical worksheet. Because the best stories don't just inspire — they transform how we lead, speak, and show up.

Whether you're leading thousands or leading quietly from within — this book is your story vault.

Please open it, and take whatever you need.

— from Your Coach,
Shannon

How to Use This Book

This is not a book to read once and put away. It's a vault to return to — again and again — until the stories inside become yours.

Each chapter is designed to help you internalize a powerful leadership moment and speak from it when it matters. Here's how to get the most from every chapter:

Step-by-Step Practice

1. Read the Story Aloud — Several Times.

Speak it out. Let the rhythm, tone, and structure settle into your voice.

2. Review the Expressions.

Check the used expressions. Look up what you need. Practice using them in new contexts.

3. Reflect Using the Worksheet.

Answer the prompts with honesty. Speak your thoughts out loud. This is where your leadership voice starts to emerge.

4. Cover the Story — and Try to Retell It.

This is the most powerful part. **Hide the main text. Look only at the hints.** *Then,* **try to reconstruct the story from memory — out loud.**

Visualize the situation as if it were your own. Tell it like it happened to you.

And if you forget an exact sentence or stumble on a word? Don't worry.

Keep going — in your words, your way. *The goal isn't perfect recall. It's authentic delivery.*

5. Repeat Until It Becomes Yours.

Go back, refine, retell. When you can confidently deliver the story as your own — not just in words but in presence — then move on to the next chapter.

By the end of this book, you will have loaded your mind with **11 compelling stories** *— each ready to be told (or adapted) in real business moments. Some you may use verbatim. Others will simply live in your voice as material for smart improvisation.*

However you use them — **Own them. Speak them. Make them yours**.

You've got this.

Table of Contents

Chapter 01	The Leadership Narrative Effect	009
Chapter 02	The Art of Eliciting the Truth	019
Chapter 03	What Are You Building For?	028
Chapter 04	Focus on the Signal	037
Chapter 05	Why I Still Read Books in the Age of AI	047
Chapter 06	Leading with Beginner's Mind	057
Chapter 07	The Animal in the Room	067
Chapter 08	When the Problem Isn't the Problem	077
Chapter 09	The Voice Inside the Leader	087
Chapter 10	The Leader's Shortcut to Peak Performance	097
Chapter 11	Becoming the Leader Your Future Needs	107

Chapter 01

THE LEADERSHIP NARRATIVE EFFECT

When to Use Town Hall Meetings, Leadership Offsites, 1:1 Coaching Conversations

Para. 1 ▶ **Hint** Opening with a realization about self-narratives

Not long ago, I found myself listening to an interview featuring Vanessa Van Edwards, and something she said landed like a ton of bricks.

She talked about how each of us lives by a "self-narrative" — a kind of internal storyline about who we are and how we became that way.

One of the most empowering ones, she said, is the hero narrative: "I've worked hard, made mistakes, learned, and grown."

That idea really made me pause.

What's the story I've been telling myself all these years? And more importantly — how is that narrative shaping the way I lead others?

▶ self-narrative, hero narrative, the story we tell ourselves

Para. 2 ▶ **Hint** Introducing the healer and victim narratives and applying them to the workplace

She also introduced two other types: the healer and the victim. Healers often put others before themselves, usually because they were put in a position of caretaking early on. Their value is tied to being helpful — even at the expense of their own needs. I've met amazing team players like that, but sometimes they say yes too often and burn out fast. Victims, on the other hand, tend to think the world is stacked against them. No matter how smart or hardworking they are, they don't feel lucky — and that perception quietly drains their motivation and creativity. Recognizing these patterns in ourselves and our teams can really change the way we lead.

▶ put a before b, put sth last, be put in a position of, caretaking, people-pleaser, victim narrative

Para. 3 ▶ **Hint** Sharing the "luck perception" experiment and its leadership meaning

---

Vanessa asked a simple but powerful question: "Do you feel lucky?"

She shared a fascinating study where participants were asked to count images in a newspaper.

On page two, a big sign read: "Stop counting. There are 42 images."

The kicker? People who thought of themselves as lucky spotted it right away.

Those who didn't — kept counting and missed the opportunity.

It was a striking reminder that our perception of luck shapes what we notice… or don't.

▶ do you feel lucky, think of A as B, kicker, perception of

Para. 4 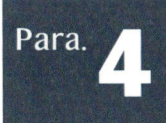 ▶ **Hint** Highlighting how energy and performance spread in teams

Later in the same talk, she shared a study that floored me.

After analyzing over 58,000 working hours across 11 companies, researchers found this:

If you sit within 25 feet of a high performer, your own performance can improve by 15%.

But here's the kicker — if you sit near a low performer, it can decrease by 30%.

That made me think about the unspoken cues we send and receive every day.

As leaders, we have a responsibility to curate the emotional climate we're part of.

▶ improve by, decrease by, cue, kicker, contagious

| Para. 5 | ▶ Hint | Closing with a personal takeaway and small leadership habit |

Since hearing that, I've been more intentional about the cues I give off — especially when things aren't going as planned.

Even something as small as how I respond in a tense meeting or how I walk into a room… it matters.

And when I coach younger colleagues, I remind them that they don't need a big speech or a grand victory to become a hero.

Sometimes, all it takes is one small moment of heroism — saying what you really think, offering help without being asked, or simply believing that change is possible — to start rewriting your story.

▶ cue, small moment of heroism, think of A as B, growth mindset

▶ **Quick Summary Box**

The Three Self-Narratives

Narrative Type	Core Belief	Typical Traits	Risk in Leadership
Hero	"I grow through effort."	Resilient, accountable, inspiring	May push too hard without reflection
Healer	"My value is in helping."	Empathetic, service-driven, people-pleaser	Risk of burnout, saying yes too often
Victim	"The world is against me."	Cynical, defensive, self-doubting	May resist change or feedback

▶ **Leadership Reflection Box**

Ask Yourself

- What's my default self-narrative under pressure?
- Do I see opportunities—or do I feel they're meant for someone else?
- What subtle cues am I sending my team about resilience, optimism, or fear?

WORKSHEET

step 1   **Identify Your Narrative**

◆ What's your current self-narrative?

(Check one that most resonates with how you usually think about yourself.)

Hero : "I've overcome challenges with effort and resilience."

Healer: "I'm valuable when I help others, even at my own cost."

Victim: "No matter how hard I try, things don't go my way."

Reflect:

In what kinds of situations does this narrative show up most clearly in your leadership?

step 2   Spot the Cues You are Sending

❖ What kind of **nonverbal or verbal cues** do you think you send during the following situations?

Situation	Possible Cue I Give Off	Desired Cue Instead
When I'm under stress	e.g.) short answers, silence	e.g.) calm tone, direct framing
When someone makes a mistake	e.g.) sighs, fixing it myself	e.g.) coaching moment
In team meetings		

step 3   Micro-Heroism Challenge

❖ List **one small moment of heroism** you will commit to this week:

(It can be as small as saying "no" to something that doesn't align with your priorities, or giving unexpected positive feedback.)

step 4   Who's in Your 25-Foot Zone?

◆ Write the names of 3-5 people you work most closely with. Do their energy and mindset **lift** or **drain** you?

Name	Lift / Drain?	What's one action I can take?

step 5   Reframe Your Script

◆ Complete the following sentence:

"I used to think of myself as someone who _____, but now I'm learning to think of myself as someone who ____ _____."

Chapter 02

THE ART OF ELICITING THE TRUTH

When to Use High-Stakes Meetings, Negotiations, Performance Reviews

Para. 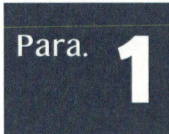 ▶ Hint   Discovery of a CIA-origin technique called elicitation — surprisingly useful in business.

I recently came across an interview with a behavioral expert named Chase Hughes, and something he said really stayed with me.

He was talking about a communication technique called elicitation — something originally developed in intelligence circles, but surprisingly relevant in business.

The idea is simple but powerful: instead of asking direct questions, which can sometimes make people put their guard up,

you guide the conversation using statements that naturally lead the other person to share information.

And they don't even realize they're doing it.

▶ elicitation, get one's guard up, communication technique

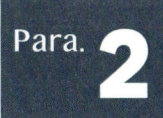 **Para. 2** ▶ **Hint** The Whole Foods salary example — correction triggers disclosure.

One example really stuck with me. Hughes described a scenario where someone makes a deliberate false statement like,

"I heard everyone at your company just got a raise to $26 an hour."

The other person instinctively corrects it — "No, actually, I make $17" — and in doing so, gives up information they probably wouldn't have shared if asked directly.

That simple shift — from pressing to provoking correction — felt like a subtle kind of leadership superpower.

▶ come up with, get bumped up to, be pressed, give up information, correct the record

Para. 3 ▶ **Hint** Reflection — I used to press, now I use soft statements and people open up.

That made me think about some of my own interactions — whether with clients, partners, or internal reviews.

I realized I often tend to press for answers, especially when I need clarity fast.

But sometimes that can unintentionally shut people down.

What I've started trying instead is striking up a more casual conversation and using soft statements like,

"I bet that project had its fair share of challenges."

The results have been surprising. People open up. They feel heard. And I actually learn more — with less effort.

▶ press for answers, strike up a conversation, I bet, give up details

▶ **Hint** Rule of thumb — the more sensitive the topic, the fewer questions.

One key rule of thumb I took away from that interview was this:

The more sensitive or high-stakes the information, the fewer direct questions you should ask.

It's about building rapport and lowering resistance. It's subtle — but in leadership, nuance often matters more than force.

▶ rule of thumb, high-stakes, fewer questions, lowering resistance

Para. 5 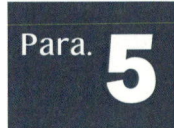 ▶ **Hint** Takeaway — listen more, elicit more — not everything needs to be asked.

So now, whenever I walk into a negotiation, a boardroom, or even a tricky performance review,

I remind myself: listen more, assume less, and let the conversation work for you.

Communication isn't just about what we ask — it's about what we elicit.

And often, the best insights come not when you question harder, but when you speak softer.

▶ elicit, let the conversation work, speak softer, assume less

▶ **Quick Summary Box**

The Layers of Elicitation

Layer of Elicitation	Technique	Example Statement	Outcome
1. Correction	Deliberate False Statement	"You guys all got a raise to $26, right?"	"No, I actually make $17."
2. Suggestion	Empathetic / Soft Assumption	"I bet that wasn't easy to pull off."	Person opens up with story or details.
3. Disbelief	Provoking Clarification via Doubt	"No way had that gone 100% smooth."	"Well… actually, the first two days…"

▶ **Leadership Reflection Box**

Ask Yourself

- When do I tend to press too hard in conversation?
- What soft statements could I use instead of questions?
- Who on my team shuts down when asked too directly — and how can I elicit more instead of ask more?

WORKSHEET

step 1 | **Recall a Time You Pressed for Information**

◆ What was the outcome? Did the person open up or shut down?

Situation: _____

My approach: _____

Result: _____

step 2 | **Reframe It Using Elicitation**

◆ How could you rephrase that same interaction using one of the 3 elicitation layers?

Elicitation Layer	New Statement
Correction	"I heard you all agree it's a done deal."
Suggestion	"I imagine that took a lot of back-and-forth."
Disbelief	"No way that got unanimous approval, right?"

step 3 Build a Go-To Phrase List

◆ Write 2–3 elicitation-style statements you can use in upcoming conversations.

1.

2.

3.

step 4 Apply This Week

◆ In what meeting or conversation will you consciously avoid asking questions — and try elicitation instead?

Context: _____

What I'll try: _____

Chapter 03

WHAT ARE YOU BUILDING FOR?

When to Use Strategic Planning Sessions, Founder Retreats, AI Ethics Discussions

Para. 1 ▶ **Hint** Realization — AI is not just completing tasks, it's starting to complete thoughts.

I was recently struck by a powerful insight from Brendan McCord, founder of the Cosmos Institute.

He warned that as AI continues to evolve, we'll face an unprecedented temptation — the temptation to outsource our thinking.

What began as convenience — email sorting, music recommendations — is moving into the realm of decision-making, value-setting, and even life purpose.

Are we entering an age of "autocomplete for life"?

That question hit me hard.

▶ outsource thinking, autocomplete for life, in the realm of

Para. 2 ▶ **Hint** The danger — when builders stop asking why.

McCord described three types of builders we should be wary of.

The Puzzle Absorbed are obsessed with solving technical problems but forget to ask what the problems are for.

The Reductionists believe if something can't be solved by computation, it isn't worth solving at all.

And the Dismissers — well, they think philosophy is irrelevant in an age of code.

The irony? That belief itself is a weak philosophical position.

And in my industry, I've met all three.

▶ puzzle absorbed, reductionist, dismissers, is it worth V-ing at all?

Para. 3 ▶ **Hint** Inspiration — Franklin as the philosopher-builder.

What McCord offers as an antidote is what he calls the philosopher-builder — someone who marries technical innovation with moral imagination.

Benjamin Franklin was his example. Franklin mastered the technologies of his time, from bifocals to lightning rods.

But he also lived by 13 virtues and translated Enlightenment ideas into public institutions like the library and Constitution.

He didn't just ask how — he asked why.

And that's the kind of leader I aspire to be.

▶ philosopher-builder, marry A with B, prolific, virtue, translate into

Para. 4 ▶ Hint A caution — are we hollowing out the human role in decision-making?

McCord's deeper worry is that as AI gets stronger, it may not just support our choices — it might silently replace them.

He calls this the risk of being hollowed out — a world where our agency is quietly eroded by the tools we built to serve us.

The next trillion dollars in AI will either expand human autonomy — or automate it away.

That's the real leadership challenge: are we building tools that strengthen self-direction, or eliminate the need for it?

▶ hollowed out, human autonomy, automation vs. agency

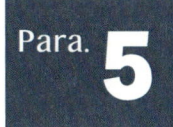

▶ Hint   Leadership shift — from builder to guide.

That's why I've started asking myself a new kind of question — not just "What am I building?" but "What am I building for?"

And that small change has made a big difference.

It forces me to step back, tease out assumptions, and remember that leadership is not just propulsion — it's also guidance.

In this age of acceleration, taking time to reflect is not a luxury.

It's the star tracker we desperately need.

▶ what am I building for, tease out, propulsion, guidance, step back

▶ **Quick Summary Box**

Building with Purpose

Concept	Definition / Example	Why It Matters
Autocomplete for Life	AI shaping thoughts and choices without awareness	Threatens autonomy and decision-making
Puzzle Absorbed	Technologists solving without reflection	May produce powerful but purposeless systems
Philosopher-Builder	Technologist who blends wisdom with execution	Anchors innovation in human flourishing
Franklin Model	Philosophy translated into practical tools	Proves idea and impact can co-exist
"What am I building for?"	Purpose-first mindset for leaders	Keeps vision grounded amid fast growth

▶ **Leadership Reflection Box**

Ask Yourself

- Am I only asking "How?" — or do I regularly ask "Why?"

- Do my products, tools, or systems strengthen or bypass human agency?

- What personal or team rituals help me reconnect with first principles?

WORKSHEET

step 1 Define Your Current Role

❖ What are you actively building, managing, or leading right now?

My current work involves _____

step 2 Apply the Franklin Filter

❖ Ask: Is this only technically impressive — or philosophically meaningful too?

Task / Project	Technically Sound?	Human Purpose it Serves?

step 3 Spot the Archetype You Lean Toward

❖ Be honest — which mindset do you fall into during crunch time?

Puzzle Absorbed: "Let me solve it first, ask why later."

Reductionist: "Only data matters."

Dismisser: "We don't have time for philosophy."

step 4   **Reframe Your Next Build**

◆ Rewrite one initiative with purpose-first framing.

Instead of: "How do we scale this fast?"
Try: "What human needs are we scaling — and why?"

step 5   **Choose One Weekly Reflection Ritual**

◆ Ideas: A silent 10-minute walk before decision-making. A Monday journaling prompt. A quote above your screen.

My ritual will be: _____

Chapter 04

FOCUS ON THE SIGNAL

When to Use Time Management, Prioritization, Stress Management, Productivity Coaching Moments

Para.  ▶ Hint   Realization — Starting with an idea that sparked reflection

I once heard Kevin O'Leary say something that completely reframed the way I approach leadership.

He was talking about Steve Jobs and how he managed his time—not by thinking in years or even months,

but by identifying the top 3 to 5 things he had to get done in the next 18 hours.

Everything else was noise.

That idea hit me hard—because I realized I was letting way too much noise into my day.

▶ get done, noise, leadership, reframe the way I approach

Para. 2 ▶ **Hint** Quoting the signal-to-noise ratio idea and personal adoption

Jobs operated on what he called a "signal-to-noise ratio." For him, 80% of his energy was on signal—those top critical tasks.

The remaining 20% was noise, and he fiercely protected his time.

When I looked at my own schedule, I realized I was hovering around a 50/50 ratio on most days.

So I made a shift.

Now, every morning, I deem just three things as truly critical—and I don't let anything distract me from getting those done.

▶ signal-to-noise ratio, deem, distract me from

Para. 3 ▶ **Hint** Noting the emotional reality of entrepreneurship

Of course, business isn't clean or predictable.

You face the ebb and flow—a failed deal at 10 AM, a breakthrough at 11.

I've had mornings where I lose a key partner and afternoons where I close a deal that changes our trajectory.

But here's what I remind myself: the emotion is noise.

The signal doesn't change.

And as Steve Jobs told O'Leary, "Focus on the signal. That's it."

▶ ebb and flow, focus on the signal

Para. 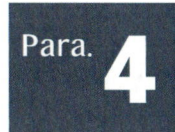 ▶ Hint   Making room for creative balance without compromising signal

That doesn't mean I live like a machine.

Jobs might've been 80/20, but Elon Musk is 100% signal—and honestly, that's not for me.

I've come to believe in what O'Leary called the yin and yang of leadership:

clarity and execution during work hours, creativity and rest outside of them.

Late at night, I unwind with jazz guitar or long walks—because I need that balance.

But I never confuse leisure for priority. Signal comes first.

▶ yin and yang, balance, signal comes first

Para. 5 ▶ **Hint** Tying it back to a mantra or leadership habit

Now, when I walk into the office, I already know my three.

I don't check email first. I don't scroll.

I protect those 18 hours—and my team knows it too.

Signal-first leadership has made me extraordinarily more focused and effective.

It's not always easy—but it is simple.

And that simplicity has changed how I lead, how I live, and how I win.

▶ extraordinarily, protect my time, signal-first leadership

▶ **Quick Summary Box**

Building with Purpose

Key Idea	Description
Signal-to-Noise Ratio	Prioritize 3–5 essential tasks each day and eliminate distractions
Emotional Resilience	Don't let emotions or unexpected events pull you off your signal
Balance with Intent	Practice the yin and yang—deep focus during work, creativity after hours
Practical Impact	Improved focus, productivity, and clarity in daily leadership
Core Mantra	"Focus on the signal. That's it."

▶ **Leadership Reflection Box**

Ask Yourself

- Are you clear on what your "signal" is today?
- How much of your calendar is being taken up by "noise"?
- What boundaries can you set to protect your most productive hours?
- Do you give yourself permission to unplug after your critical tasks are done?

WORKSHEET

step 1   **Daily Signal Audit**

◆ What are the top 3 things you must get done in the next 18 hours?

1.

2.

3.

step 2   **Identify the Noise**

◆ Ask: What distractions commonly pull you away from those top 3?

step 3   Create a Signal Block

◆ Choose your most focused 2-hour block each day. Name it and claim it.

<small>e.g., "My Morning Signal Hours: 8AM–10AM"Puzzle
Absorbed: "Let me solve it first, ask why later."</small>

Time: _____

Rules: _____

step 4   Emotional Recalibration

◆ Think of a recent day where things went up and down. What was your signal that day?

Chaos happened: _____

How I stayed (or didn't stay) on signal: _____

step 5   **Personal Mantra Rewrite**

❖ Write your own variation of "Focus on the signal" to post somewhere visible.

"_____"

Chapter 05

WHY I STILL READ BOOKS IN THE AGE OF AI?

When to Use Leadership Development Sessions, Town Hall Meetings, Strategic Reflection on Identity and Growth

Para. 1 ▶ **Hint**   Starting with an idea that sparked reflection

Not long ago, I read something by Dan Koe that really challenged my thinking.

He said most people treat reading as a performative act—we read to check boxes, impress others, or feel like we're making progress.

But we often miss out on the deeper reason for reading: to change who we are.

That line hit me.

It made me reflect not just on how I read, but why I read at all—especially as a leader.

▶ performative act, miss out on, make progress on

Para. 2 ▶ **Hint** Connecting reading to leadership and behavior change

Koe makes a compelling point: we don't read to find specific answers anymore—that's what Google or ChatGPT is for.

Instead, he argues that real reading requires a fundamental rewiring of the mind.

Not just accumulating information, but becoming someone new.

In leadership, we often look for actionable steps, checklists, or quick fixes.

But what really moves us forward?

It's often a new way of seeing, not just a new thing to do.

▶ requires a fundamental rewiring of, actionable steps, a new way of seeing

Para. 3 ▶ **Hint** Raising the "identity vs information" dilemma

Dan calls out the elephant in the room: AI gives us endless information at the tip of our fingers,

but the problem isn't information—it's identity.

You can spit out facts all day, but if your identity hasn't shifted, your actions won't either.

And that really resonates.

I've met brilliant people who know all the right strategies,

but they never quite take the leap—because they're still the same person inside.

Leadership, to me, is often about *shifting identity first*.

▶ elephant in the room, at the tip of their fingers, identity problem, spit out

Para. 4 ▶ **Hint**   Personal shift from summaries to deep books

---

I'll admit it—there was a time I swapped real reading for brain rot summaries.

Quick videos, condensed blog posts, AI summaries... I thought I was being efficient.

But something felt shallow.

Now, I find the richest insights in the books AI wouldn't even think to summarize.

A 400-page history of failure, or a memoir with no clear "lesson"—that's where the gold is.

They stretch my thinking.

They give me a new angle to view things from—especially tough decisions.

▶ swap A for B, that's where the gold is, give sb a new angle to view sth from

Para. 5 ▶ **Hint** Tying back to leadership and practice

Since then, I've changed how I recommend books to others.

I don't suggest what's trending or "high ROI."

Instead, I say: read what doesn't make sense right away.

Read what challenges you.

Because in leadership, just like in reading, the point isn't to look smart.

The point is to become someone wiser.

And sometimes, that starts with a page no algorithm would ever pick for you.

▶ read what challenges you, not to look smart, become someone wiser

▶ **Quick Summary Box**

Key Message	Example Expression
Most people read to appear productive, not to transform.	performative act, make progress on
AI gives us information, but doesn't change our identity.	elephant in the room, identity problem
Real growth comes from deep, challenging, even impractical books.	that's where the gold is, swap A for B
Leaders must read not for answers, but for new perspectives.	give sb a new angle to view sth from, become someone wiser
Most people read to appear productive, not to transform.	performative act, make progress on

▶ **Leadership Reflection Box**

- Do I read to find solutions, or to find myself?
- When was the last time a book truly shifted my perspective as a leader?
- Am I defaulting to summaries and bullet points—and what might I be missing because of that?
- How can I encourage my team to read in a way that rewires how they think, not just what they know?

WORKSHEET

step 1   **Self Check**

◆ I usually read:

☐ To find quick solutions

☐ To broaden my perspective

☐ To appear productive

☐ To reflect and evolve

step 2   **Identify a Reading Habit to Break**

◆ What shallow reading habit do I want to stop?

e.g.: Overreliance on summaries, skimming only leadership bestsellers, etc.

step 3   Choose a Stretch Book

♦ Pick one book that doesn't directly relate to your job but expands your thinking.

Title: _____

step 4   Reflect After Reading

♦ What belief or assumption did this book challenge?

♦ What is one new "angle" I gained that I couldn't have Googled?

step 5   Leadership Application

◆ How might this new idea influence how I lead, decide, or mentor others?

Chapter 06

LEADING WITH BEGINNER'S MIND

When to Use Leadership Retreats, Mindfulness Workshops, Change Management Conversations

Para. 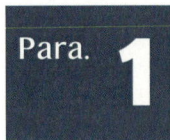 ▶ **Hint** Discovery — Zen offers a fresh lens for leading in uncertainty.

I've always admired leaders who seem grounded—calm in the middle of chaos.

Recently, I came across a talk by Robert Waldinger, a Harvard professor and Zen Master, and it completely reframed how I think about presence, control, and leadership.

Zen, he says, isn't about escaping the world—it's about seeing it clearly.

Its wisdom doesn't just belong in meditation halls. It belongs in boardrooms too.

▶ Zen, reframed, presence, leadership lens

Para. 2 ▶ **Hint** Impermanence — letting go of control can be a relief.

One of Zen's core teachings is impermanence—the idea that nothing is fixed.

On the one hand, that can be disorienting. On the other, it's freeing.

I've realized how much time I spend trying to hold onto what's no longer true:

a strategy that used to work, a team structure that once fit, a version of myself I no longer am.

Letting go of that fixed view makes room for what's next.

It doesn't make change easy—but it does make it workable.

▶ impermanence, there's nothing fixed, hold onto, fixed view, workable

Para. 3 ▶ **Hint**   Suffering — stories we add to pain amplify it.

Zen doesn't promise the end of pain—but it helps us stop layering extra suffering on top.

Like when something goes wrong at work, and I start spinning stories:

"They don't respect me," or "I'm failing," or "This always happens."

But when I pause and just feel the discomfort—without judgment—it passes more cleanly.

Leadership is full of challenges. We can't eliminate pain.

But we can reduce how much we multiply it.

▶ suffering, in a way that, stories we tell ourselves, what's going on in me

Para. 4  ▶ **Hint** Mindfulness — being here, now, fully.

Waldinger offered my favorite definition of mindfulness:

"Paying attention in the present moment without judgment."

That sounds simple, but in my experience, it's radical.

The feel of the room during a tense meeting. The way someone's tone changes.

Even my own breath, when I remember to check in.

When I practice this — even for a minute — I make better decisions.

And I relate to people from awareness, not autopilot.

▶ mindfulness, present moment, stimuli, without judgment

Para. 5 ▶ Hint   Beginner's Mind — humility unlocks innovation.

The Zen concept that changed me most was Beginner's Mind:

Letting go of what we think we know, and approaching things with curiosity.

It reminded me of something Shunryu Suzuki once said:

> "In the beginner's mind, there are many possibilities. In the expert's mind, there are few."

That quote now lives on my desk.

Because when I pause the expert in me and listen with humility, new insights often arise—ones I would've missed if I assumed I already knew what's what.

▶ beginner's mind, we know what's what, arise, curiosity, expert vs. beginner

▶ **Quick Summary Box**

Zen Teachings for Modern Leaders

Concept	Zen Insight	Leadership Application
Impermanence	Nothing is fixed. Change is constant.	Let go of rigid plans; stay adaptable.
Suffering	We amplify pain with our stories.	Pause narrative, lead with clarity.
Mindfulness	Nothing is fixed. Change is constant.	Notice team dynamics and act intentionally.

▶ **Leadership Reflection Box**

Ask Yourself

- What am I holding onto that no longer serves me or my team?
- When do I resist change because of fear—not facts?
- How often do I lead from clarity, rather than from internal narrative or noise?
- What might become possible if I practiced beginner's mind in a key decision?

WORKSHEET

step 1   Notice Your Storylines

◆ Think of a recent work challenge. What story did you tell yourself?

Situation: _____

My approach: _____

Result: _____

step 2   Practice Present Awareness

◆ Set a 1-minute timer. In silence, list what you notice right now:

Situation: _____

My approach: _____

Thoughts (without judgment): _____

step 3   **Apply Beginner's Mind**

◆ Choose one ongoing project or team issue. List three questions you could ask from a place of curiosity—not certainty.

1.

2.

3.

step 4   **Release a Fixed View**

◆ Identify a preference or belief you're holding too tightly. Reframe it:

"I used to think of myself as someone who _____, but now I'm learning to think of myself as someone who __ _____."

step 5   Daily Anchor Phrase

◆ Choose a sentence to ground your week. Here are examples:

"Everything is workable."

"Let go of knowing."

"Lead from presence."

My phrase: _____.

Chapter 07

THE ANIMAL IN THE ROOM

When to Use   Performance Reviews, Team-Building Workshops, Conflict Resolution Moments

Para. 1 ▶ **Hint** Realization — not every power dynamic is what it seems.

A while back, I listened to former Secret Service agent Evy Poumpouras explain how people show up as one of four animal-based personality archetypes: Lion, T-Rex, Mouse, or Monkey.

At first, it sounded like a fun framework — but the more I thought about it, the more I realized how often we misread people by looking at what they say instead of how they behave.

She made one point that really stuck with me: "If you want to read people well — shut up."

Watch. Listen. People show you who they are.

▶ archetype, shut up, read people, show you who they are

Para. 2 ▶ **Hint** Understanding the four types — and how they shift.

Lions like to set the agenda. T-Rexes speak their mind — sometimes too directly.

Mice tend to stay quiet, aiming to fit in or avoid conflict.

And Monkeys? They're the warm, social, energetic ones — the life of the meeting.

But here's the key: we don't have just one mode.

I've seen colleagues who are Lions at work turn into Mice at home.

Or a Monkey at the coffee machine become a T-Rex under pressure.

Context changes character. And awareness is everything.

▶ lion, t-rex, mouse, monkey, come off, flip, suppress

Para. 3 ▶ **Hint**   There are good versions — and bad ones.

Each type has a helpful version and a harmful one.

A good Lion leads with clarity. A bad one bullies.

A good T-Rex is assertive and honest. A bad one turns punitive or dogmatic.

Mice can be humble listeners — or overly submissive.

Monkeys can be inclusive hosts — or pushy attention-seekers.

I've learned to ask myself not just, "Who am I in this meeting?"

but also, "Am I being the good version of that?"

▶ forthright, submissive, avoidant, dogmatic, punitive, keep in check

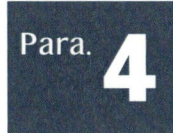 ▶ **Hint** Using type-awareness to lead more effectively.

When I walk into a room now, I try to spot the animal in the room — not to stereotype, but to tune in.

If I'm managing a Mouse, I slow down, create safety, invite their voice.

With a Monkey, I stay warm but set boundaries early.

If a T-Rex is pushing hard, I check if it's courage or combat.

And when dealing with Lions, I ask myself: do they want control, or just clarity?

It's not about labeling — it's about leading with empathy.

▶ read the room, boundaries, tuning in, lead with empathy, delegate with type-awareness

Para. 5 ▶ **Hint** Self-awareness makes the system work.

Ultimately, the real power of this framework is personal.

We can't choose our instincts — but we can choose our response.

I know I lean T-Rex when things get intense. I want to fight.

But now I catch myself and ask: what does this moment need?

A sharp push? Or a calm hand?

The best leaders I know don't just understand others — they keep themselves in check.

They lead the animal within, before they try to lead the room.

▶ instincts, keep in check, come off, lead the room, lead the self

▶ **Quick Summary Box**

Animal Archetypes in Leadership

Arche-type	Good Version	Bad Version	Needs from Others
Lion	Decisive, clear, agenda-setting	Overcontrolling, dominating	Respect and room to lead
T-Rex	Honest, competitive, assertive	Combative, sarcastic, dogmatic	Directness with respect
Mouse	Humble, observant, adaptable	Overly submissive, avoidant	Psychological safety and invitation
Monkey	Warm, social, high-energy	istracting, overly eager, boundary-crossing	Structure, inclusion, and light boundaries

▶ **Leadership Reflection Box**

Ask Yourself

- What archetype do I most often default to under pressure?
- When do I slip into the "bad version" of my type?
- Who on my team tends to flip personalities in different contexts — and how can I support them?
- How can I use this awareness to communicate more effectively this week?

WORKSHEET

step 1   Identify Your Primary Archetype at Work

❖ Which animal type describes you best in your work environment?

☐ Lion
☐ T-Rex
☐ Mouse
☐ Monkey

Example behavior I've shown: _____

step 2   Reflect on Your "Bad Version" Moments

❖ When have you acted from the negative side of your archetype?

Situation: _____

What triggered me: _____

How could I have responded differently? _____

step 3 — Personality Map Your Team (Confidential Exercise)

◆ Write down key team members and their likely archetype.

Name	Likely Archetype	One way to support them effectively

step 4 — Type-Aware Delegation

◆ Choose one task you're delegating soon. How can you assign or present it based on personality fit?

Task: _____

Who is best fit for it & why: _____

step 5   Anchor Statement for the Week

♦ Choose a phrase to help you stay in the "good version" of your archetype.

"Direct is good. Dogmatic is not."

"Listen before I lead."

"Warmth with boundaries."

My phrase: _____.

Chapter 08

WHEN THE PROBLEM ISN'T THE PROBLEM

When to Use Difficult Conversations, Conflict Mediation, Team Dynamics Coaching

 ▶ **Hint** Realization — one bad interaction can ripple far beyond the moment.

I used to think, "It's just work — we don't have to like everyone."

But after years of experience (and a few bruises), I've realized how wrong that framing is.

Amy Gallo put it best: "One negative interaction with a colleague can be detrimental to your mental health and your career."

That made me rethink how I approach the people who push my buttons — not just as annoyances, but as leadership tests.

▶ push one's buttons, detrimental, it doesn't have to be that way

Para. 2 ▶ **Hint** Passive-aggressive behavior isn't always intentional — it's fear in disguise.

One of the trickiest patterns I've faced is the passive-aggressive peer — the person who smiles and says "I'm fine," but whose tone or follow-through says otherwise.

Gallo points out that these behaviors often stem from fear — fear of conflict, rejection, or failure.

The solution isn't calling it out harshly. It's making space.

Space for them to express, clarify, articulate what they can't quite say directly.

▶ passive-aggressive, say one thing then do another, what's underneath that, allow room for, articulate

Para. 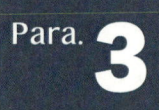 ▶ **Hint**   Insecure bosses don't just hurt others — they erode your self-belief.

At one point, I reported to an insecure boss who micromanaged everything I did.

I started questioning myself more than they questioned me.

Gallo suggests pointing out their strengths — sincerely.

In my case, I acknowledged their knack for spotting risk early, and it diffused tension.

It's not about flattery. It's about anchoring their confidence so they can step back.

▶ insecure, micromanage, question oneself, point out, appreciate

Para. 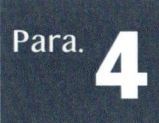 ▶ **Hint** The tormentor archetype — when mentors become rivals.

Then there's the tormentor — the person who should lift you up but seems intent on proving you're not cut out for the role.

I've had that happen too. And it's destabilizing.

Gallo's advice? Show that you're invested in their success.

Not as a strategy of submission, but of survival.

If they stop seeing you as a threat, they may stop trying to undermine you.

▶ tormentor, be cut out for, lift sb up, show investment, alter the dynamic

Para. 5 ▶ **Hint** The first place to start is always with yourself.

What I appreciate most from Gallo's approach is this:

you can't control their mindset — only yours.

Before acting, she advises doing some reflection:

Why is this bothering me so much? What's my role in the dynamic?

That internal work has become my habit because changing how I respond often changes the interaction altogether.

▶ the first place to start is, do some reflection, have a strong reaction to, lay the groundwork, alter the dynamic

▶ **Quick Summary Box**

Three Difficult Archetypes and How to Respond

Archetype	Behavior Pattern	Constructive Response
Passive-Aggressive	Indirect communication, hidden frustration	Create safety, allow room to clarify, don't label
Insecure Boss	Micromanagement, subtle control	Sincerely point out strengths, ground their confidence
Tormentor	Undermining disguised as mentorship	Invest in their success, reduce perceived threat

▶ **Leadership Reflection Box**

Ask Yourself

- Who is one colleague that I currently have tension with — and which archetype might they reflect?
- What about their behavior triggers me most — and why?
- Have I been trying to change them, or shifting how I respond to them?
- What fear might be driving their actions?

WORKSHEET

step 1 — Map the Conflict

◆ Choose a recent tension. Label it using the archetypes.

Person: _____

Archetype: _____

Key behavior observed: _____

step 2 — Pause and Reflect

◆ What's my honest emotional reaction?

I felt: _____

Why might that be?: _____

step 3 — Choose a Reframe Strategy

♦ Select one tactic below and write how you might apply it.

- ☐ Create space for honest expression
- ☐ Point out a genuine strength
- ☐ Reaffirm shared goals or respect
- ☐ Decrease my defensiveness or need for control

Tactic I'll try: _____

step 4 — Model the Behavior You Want to See

♦ Rewrite how you'll approach the next interaction.

Instead of: "They need to stop undermining me,"
Try: "I'll enter the conversation with calm curiosity and set a clearer tone."

step 5 Anchor Phrase

♦ Choose a sentence to guide your approach.

Examples:

"Their reaction is about them — my response is about me."

"Make room, not war."

"Respond, don't react."

My phrase: _____

Chapter 09

THE VOICE INSIDE THE LEADER

When to Use Solo Decision-Making, High-Stakes Presentations, Crisis Leadership Moments

Para. 1 ▶ **Hint** Realization — how we talk to ourselves becomes how we lead others.

One morning, I caught myself muttering, "You always mess this up," after misplacing my keys.

It wasn't a big deal — but the tone caught my attention.

If I spoke to a teammate like that, I'd consider it unacceptable.

So why speak to myself that way?

That's when I started digging into the science of self-talk — and what I found changed the way I lead.

▶ self-talk, every single day, push one's buttons, the way you talk to yourself

Para. 2 ▶ **Hint** Self-talk shapes our energy, resilience, and clarity.

Psychologists define self-talk as verbalized thoughts directed toward ourselves.

It includes motivational statements ("You've got this"), neutral reflections ("That didn't go well"), and — unfortunately — harsh criticism.

Studies show that instructional and motivational self-talk improves focus and performance.

One reason? When our inner dialogue supports us, we show up stronger for others.

It's quiet, but it matters.

▶ define A as, fall into category, be activated, incorporate A into B

Para. 3 ▶ **Hint** Distanced self-talk helps reframe pressure.

There's a technique called distanced self-talk — where you address yourself by name, like you would a teammate.

Instead of "I'm going to mess this up," you say, "Chris, you're prepared. Breathe."

I started doing this before keynotes or intense negotiations.

It felt odd at first, but oddly grounding.

Talking to myself like a coach helped me perform like one.

▶ distanced self-talk, morph into, be cut out for, reduce stress

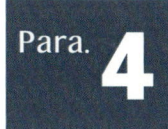

▶ Hint Negative thought cycles distort what's real.

But not all self-talk is helpful.

Over time, I noticed patterns in my thinking:

If I made one mistake, I'd catastrophize. If someone didn't respond, I'd mind read ("They must think I'm unqualified").

Cognitive behavioral therapy helped me name these habits:overgeneralization, personalization, all-or-nothing thinking.Labeling them gave me distance — and power.

▶ ruminate on, catastrophizing, overgeneralization, emotional reasoning, personalization, mind reading

Para. 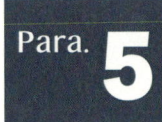 ▶ Hint   The voice you use with yourself shapes the tone of your leadership.

Today, I try to treat my inner voice like a long-term business partner —

firm, fair, and focused on improvement, not shame.

Because how we talk to ourselves doesn't stay private.

It spills into how we lead, how we listen, and how we recover.

The tone we set inside sets the tone outside.

And that's why inner leadership may be the most overlooked skill of all.

▶ internalize, lay the groundwork, tone of leadership, on one's own

▶ **Quick Summary Box**

Leading from the Inside Out

Element of Self-Talk	Description	Leadership Impact
Instructional / Motivational	Clear, kind, actionable phrases	Improves focus and confidence
Distanced Self-Talk	Speaking to yourself by name	Reduces stress, builds emotional clarity
Negative Thought Cycles	Toxic patterns like catastrophizing, mind reading	Distorts judgment and drains resilience
Cognitive Awareness	Labeling and replacing harmful patterns	Promotes calm decision-making and self-trust

▶ **Leadership Reflection Box**

Ask Yourself

- What tone does my inner voice take when I'm under pressure?
- Which negative thought cycle do I tend to fall into?
- Have I ever tried using distanced self-talk — and did it shift how I felt or performed?
- How might my self-talk be influencing how I lead my team?

WORKSHEET

step 1 — Track Your Current Self-Talk

◆ What are you actively building, managing, or leading right now?

Situation	Self-Talk Quote	Tone (Positive / Negative)

step 2 — Identify Your Thought Patterns

◆ Which of these do you notice?

- ☐ Catastrophizing
- ☐ Overgeneralization
- ☐ Emotional Reasoning
- ☐ Personalization
- ☐ "Should" Statements
- ☐ Mind Reading

Noticed Pattern _____

| step 3 | **Choose a Reframe Strategy** |

- Take a phrase you identified and rewrite it as distanced self-talk.

Original: "I'm terrible at this."

Reframed: "Dana, you're learning. Keep going."

| step 4 | **Create a Positive Cue Phrase** |

- Write one motivational or instructional cue for high-pressure moments.

Examples:

"Stay steady — one step at a time."

"You've done harder things than this."

"Lead with clarity, not perfection."

My phrase: _____

step 5 Inner Leadership Habit Tracker

◆ This week, practice positive or distanced self-talk during:

☐ 1:1 feedback session
☐ Presentation
☐ Team conflict
☐ Difficult decision
☐ End-of-day review

*Reflection: What did you notice?*_____

Chapter 10

THE LEADER'S SHORTCUT TO PEAK PERFORMANCE

When to Use Strategic Offsites, High-Focus Planning Sessions, Leadership Training Retreats

Para. 1 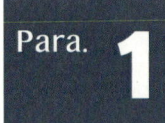 ▶ **Hint** Flow isn't magic — it's a trainable mindset.

There are days when everything clicks — when time distorts, ideas connect, and execution feels effortless.

Steven Kotler calls this the flow state, and I've come to see it as a core leadership asset.

Whether I'm presenting a vision, writing in solitude, or navigating tough negotiations, I know I'm in flow when hours go by in what feels like minutes.

It's not luck — it's preparation meeting presence.

▶ flow state, effortless effort, go by, freeze-frame, total absorption

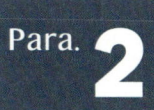

Para. 2 ▶ **Hint** Flow happens at the edge — just past comfort, not into panic.

One key to flow is what Kotler calls the challenge-skills balance —

the golden rule is to stretch but not snap.

In my leadership journey, the most engaging moments weren't easy — they were just beyond what I'd done before.

Not so hard that I panicked. Not so easy that I coasted.

As Kotler puts it, we must get good at being comfortable with being uncomfortable.

▶ golden rule to, drop into, be comfortable with being uncomfortable, stretch but not snap, push limits

Para. 3 ▶ **Hint** Focus isn't just important — it's non-negotiable.

Another flow trigger is complete concentration.

For me, this means blocking out 90–120 minutes in the morning for deep, uninterrupted work.

No meetings. No notifications. Just thinking, writing, or solving.

If I get knocked out by distraction, it can take me 15–30 minutes to get back — if I get back at all.

The quality of my leadership often depends on the protection of my attention.

▶ block out time for, get knocked out, ahead of time, at hand, distraction management

| Para. 4 | ▶ Hint | Motivation flows in sequence — curiosity → passion → purpose → autonomy → mastery. |

One of the most powerful ideas Kotler offers is the five-stage sequence of motivation.

It starts with curiosity, then deepens into passion, expands into purpose, demands autonomy, and culminates in mastery.

As I look back, that's exactly how my leadership development unfolded.

What keeps me going isn't the reward at the end — it's the intrinsic pull of progress.

Flow is what happens when that sequence aligns.

▶ intrinsic, in a sequence, from a motivation standpoint, autonomy, mastery

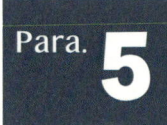

Para. 5 ▶ **Hint** Peak performance is amplified in teams — not just individuals.

Flow isn't just for solo moments.

I've witnessed group flow — when a team hits its stride, decisions become synchronized, and creativity compounds.

It doesn't happen by accident.

It requires psychological safety, aligned goals, shared rhythm, and mutual respect.

As leaders, we don't just enter flow — we design for it.

▶ group flow, perform at one's best, off the charts, commonality, across the board

▶ **Quick Summary Box**

Entering Flow as a Leader

Element	Description	Leadership Impact
Flow State	Deep immersion, altered time, total focus	Amplifies performance and insight
Challenge-Skills Balance	Task just beyond current capabilities	keeps engagement high without triggering burnout
Complete Concentration	Protected time with no distractions	Necessary for strategic work and innovation
Motivation Sequence	Curiosity → Passion → Purpose → Autonomy → Mastery	Builds long-term drive and fulfillment
Group Flow	Synchronized high performance across a team	Requires trust, rhythm, and clarity of purpose

▶ **Leadership Reflection Box**

Ask Yourself

- When was the last time I experienced personal flow — and what triggered it?
- Do I create time in my schedule for complete focus?
- Which stage of the motivation sequence am I currently in — and what comes next?
- What would it look like to design for group flow with my team this quarter?

WORKSHEET

step 1 — Define a Recent Flow Moment

- Think of a time when you felt fully immersed and energized.

    What were you doing? _____

    What made it flow-like? _____

step 2 — Apply the Challenge-Skills Balance

- What current task feels just beyond your comfort zone?

    Task: _____

    Stretch factor (1–10): _____

    One way to prepare or de-risk: _____

step 3 — Structure for Flow

◆ Block 90–120 minutes this week for deep focus. Write what you'll protect it for.

Flow Block Topic: _____

What I'll remove (distractions): _____

step 4 — Map Your Motivation Sequence

◆ *Check the stage you're in and the one you need to grow.*

☐ Curiosity
☐ Passion
☐ Purpose
☐ Autonomy
☐ Mastery

*One action to move forward:*_____

step 5   Flow as a Team

◆ Think of a project where group flow could elevate performance.

Project: _____

What would enable group flow? _____

Chapter II

BECOMING THE LEADER YOUR FUTURE NEEDS

When to Use Visioning Retreats, Executive Coaching Moments, Personal Growth Reflections

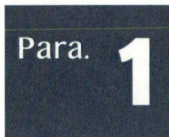

Para. 1 ▶ **Hint** Your personality shapes your reality — not the other way around.

Joe Dispenza said something I've never forgotten:

"Your personality creates your personal reality."

At first, I brushed it off as wordplay. But over time, it began to land.

If I keep thinking the same thoughts, making the same choices, feeling the same emotions —

I'll keep producing the same outcomes.

If I want a new kind of leadership life, I have to become a new kind of leader.

▶ personality creates personal reality, same thoughts same choices, modify, latch on to

Para. 2 ▶ **Hint** Change doesn't come from knowing — it comes from becoming.

Dispenza breaks it down:

Your habits become hardwired by repetition — until your body becomes your mind.

That's why we react without thinking.

By the time we're 35, most of us are running unconscious programs 95% of the time.

To change, we don't just need new knowledge.

We need to become disentangled from the identity that no longer serves us — and that takes practice, not theory.

▶ hardwired, become disentangled from, unconscious programs, payoff

Para. 3 ▶ Hint   The unknown feels uncomfortable — but that's where change lives.

Here's the hard truth: the old self feels safe because it's familiar.

Even guilt or anxiety can feel more predictable than growth.

When we start stepping into the unknown, our nervous system resists.

"I'll start tomorrow." "This isn't working." "This isn't me."

But those are just programs.

The discomfort is the door. And walking through it is where reinvention begins.

▶ get attached to, the unknown, become familiar with, step into discomfort

 **Para. 4** ▶ **Hint** Future-forward thinking can rewire your biology.

Dispenza asks: Can you believe in a future you can't yet see, but feel it so clearly your brain doesn't know the difference?

Turns out — you can.

That's what mental rehearsal does.

When done consistently, your body starts embodying your future before it arrives.

You become the vortex, not the chaser.

You stop reacting to reality — and start attracting it.

▶ visualize, emotional rehearsal, vortex, to the degree that, for an extended period of time

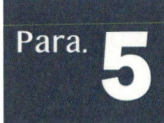

Para. 5 ▶ **Hint** Becoming isn't about results — it's about who you are when no one's watching.

There's a space Dispenza calls "the void."

It's that uncomfortable in-between when you're no longer who you were —

but not yet who you're becoming.

I've been there. Many times.

And what I've learned is this: if you can stay the course in the void,

the new version of you will start showing up.

Not all at once — but in small, consistent wins that add up.

Becoming isn't an event. It's a lifestyle.

▶ the void, add up, self-regulation, stay the course, overcome the old self

▶ **Quick Summary Box**

Inner Reprogramming for Leaders

Concept	Description	Application for Leaders
Personality = Reality	dentity shapes outcomes	Audit internal thoughts, emotions, and behaviors
Unconscious Programs	Hardwired responses from past patterns	Observe reactions, rewire over time
The Void	Transitional discomfort during transformation	Stay steady through uncertainty
Future Visualization	Emotional rehearsal of future success	Align mind and body with desired outcomes
Self-Regulation	Catching old patterns and choosing again	Cultivate conscious leadership moment to

▶ **Leadership Reflection Box**

Ask Yourself

- What version of "me" created the results I'm currently living with?
- Where in my leadership am I still running unconscious programs?
- Am I living by memories of the past — or the vision of the future?
- What's one part of my old identity I need to release?

WORKSHEET

step 1   **Observe the Old Pattern**

◆ Identify one recurring habit or emotion that reflects your old self.

Pattern: _____

When it shows up: _____

What triggers it? _____

step 2   **Visualize the Future Self**

◆ Describe a version of you who already lives in your desired future.

How do they think? _____

How do they act under pressure? _____

What emotion do they radiate daily? _____

step 3 — Rehearse the Future Emotionally

◆ Choose one moment this week where you'll mentally rehearse being that person.

Situation: _____

Visualization cue: _____

step 4 — Stay in the Unknown (The Void)

◆ What's one uncomfortable zone you're stepping into now?

Name it: _____

My new mantra in this void: _____

step 5 Track Your Wins

◆ Small shifts that prove you're becoming someone new.

Day	Micro-Victory
1.	"I paused before reacting in the meeting."
2.	"I led with clarity, not defensiveness."
3.	"I stayed calm in uncertainty."

Total Wins This Week: _____

The CEO's Story Vault (Volume 1)

Title: The CEO's Story Vault – Volume 1
Sub-title: First-Person Business Stories to Lead, Relate, and Inspire
Author: Shannon Park (박혜림)
Publisher: Collars Company Inc. (주식회사 칼라스컴퍼니)
Publishing Director: Shannon Park (박혜림)
Editor: Shannon Park (박혜림)
Design: Rachel U (유혜영)
Published Date: 2025 년 8 월 6 일
First Edition: 1st Print (2025.08.06)
Printed in: Korea
©: Shannon Park & Collars Company Inc, 2025. All rights reserved.

No part of this publication may be reproduced, distributed, or transmitted in any form or by any means, without the prior written permission of the author.

이 책의 모든 내용은 저작권법의 보호를 받습니다.
저자와 출판사의 서면동의 없이 이 책의 일부 또는 전부를 복제, 전송, 배포, 전시할 수 없습니다.

❖ 출판사 정보
Name: Collars Company Inc. (주식회사 칼라스컴퍼니)
Address: 서울시 마포구 성지 길 25-11, 지층 198 호 (합정동)
E-mail: shannon@collars.co.kr
Homepage: https://www.collars.co.kr

ISBN 979-11-982340-2-5